Making Money with Real Estate Investments

Purchase low, sell high, and beyond

Mark E. Richards

Copyright © 2023
All Rights Reserved

Table of contents

Introduction

Chapter 1

Methods for Investing in Real Estate———1

Is real estate investing right for you?———2

How much cash could you at any point contribute?———3

Is it true that you are risk open minded?———4

What are your future monetary plans?———5

Do you have the stuff?———6

How long could you at any point spend?———7

Your Most memorable Land Speculation———8

Benefitting in Land———9

Deal with Your Openness———10

Getting the Best yield———11

Trade with flawless timing———12

Setting aside Money on Seemingly insignificant details Adds Up———13

Chapter 2

The Land Deals Cycle———14

About Flipping———15

Tracking down Funding - Innovative Thoughts———16

The Bank's Point of view on Advancing Cash————17

Record of loan repayment————18

Pay history————19

Your involvement in advances————20

Current property and monetary circumstance————21

Chasing after Your Unlikely treasure————22

The Significance of the Home Assessment————23

Fixing the Property Receives Monetary Benefits————24

Arranging a Mutually beneficial Arrangement————25

Chapter 3

Different Contemplations in Effective money management———26

Know the Land Regulation———27

Contributing Expense Suggestions———28

The Advantages and disadvantages of Provincial versus Metropolitan Speculations———29

Putting resources into Land Abandonments———30

Putting resources into Business Property———31

The Upsides and downsides of Leasing Property———32

Elective Land Speculation Instruments———33

Conclusion———34

Introduction

Land financial planning is one of the most oversimplified ways of bringing in cash. With a generally little financial speculation and some perspiration value, you can turn a significant benefit. From the future point of view toward land, financial planning is positive and continually developing.

For new financial backers, one of the most troublesome obstacles to defeat is getting acquainted with everything of the land business. Land exchanges are confounded, and in the event that you are not taught on the intricate details of the business, you possibly could lose a lot of cash, quick.

Before you begin in land effective money management, invest some energy pondering the best methodology for your monetary circumstance, character, and hazard resilience.

One out of four private homes is purchased as venture property. Numerous land financial backers are customary individuals very much like you who make amazing side earnings.

Certain individuals even make to the point of making land effective money management their essential pay.

In this book, you'll find out about methodologies you can utilize while putting resources into land, the subtleties of the muddled deals process, and different focuses to consider - like land regulation, charge suggestions, and modern land speculation choices. While being a land, financial backer is, on occasion, upsetting, it likewise can be intellectually and monetarily fulfilling.

Chapter 1

Methods for Investing in Real Estate

Is real estate investing right for you?

Land is a multifaceted business that includes various lawful, monetary, and relational viewpoints. Might it be said that you are prepared to bounce into this convoluted business? Ponder these fundamental inquiries before you take your most memorable action.

How much cash could you at any point contribute?

Putting resources into the housing market requires capital. The underlying expense of money required forthright to get a property might be enormous or little. Notwithstanding, when you accept responsibility for property, you are lawfully liable for the full credit sum. Be certain you can stand to contribute by checking what is going on out. How much money do you have? What measure of obligation and how much interest could your funds at any point deal with? Contemplate the amount you can lose.

Is it true that you are risk open minded?

Hazard and capital remain inseparable. How much gamble would you say you are open to taking on? An enormous misfortune to a little financial backer has a lot bigger effect than a similar sum to a well off financial backer with abundant resources. While risk-taking can be exhilarating, speak the truth about your funds and contemplate the degree of chance that will be agreeable to you. Do you normally appreciate taking risks, or do you will quite often be more gamble antagonistically? It's fundamental to progress to realize your usual range of familiarity.

What are your future monetary plans?

Is it true that you are keen on effective financial planning to keep up with capital or to get the best yield in the briefest measure of time? Think about how much time, cash, and chance relate to every situation. Be consistent. A straight 15% benefit over two or three weeks isn't reasonable. On the off chance that you are keen on an exceptional yield, this generally implies there's more extended time responsibility, and that implies your cash will be restricted. The worth of property can change rapidly, leaving you in a higher gamble circumstance.

Do you have the stuff?

To find genuine success in land and money management, you should be meticulous, a speedy student, and have fantastic relational abilities. You really want to have the self-administration abilities expected to figure out what you want to be aware, then go out and learn it and apply it.

How long could you at any point spend?

Consider cautiously about how long you can focus on the everyday errands expected to find actual success around here. Initially, you'll have to invest a ton of energy exploring and finding out about the business. With each attempt, you'll have to invest energy taking care of on lawful problems, drafting and town issues, insurance, charge concerns, policies, statistical surveying, supporting.

Assuming that subsequent to considering these inquiries, you are as yet intrigued by land venture - congrats! This field is one of the most thrilling ways of earning enough to pay the bills.

Your Most memorable Land Speculation

Making your most memorable land exchange, either as your main living place or as an arranged venture, can be productive and energizing, yet it tends to overpower as well. Follow these means while beginning in land and money management.

1. Instruct yourself:-

This doesn't imply that you want to return to school, however you really do have to get a sense of ownership with what you really want to be aware, and learn it. Concentrate available you're keen on entering. Utilize the web, neighborhood land records, and region realtors to find the business costs of similar properties. Find out about the exchange cycle, every individual's job and obligation, the legitimate prerequisites, and protection. Every part conveys expenses that differ, and by investigating costs you can try not to lose cash.

2. Set your funding up:-

A typical mix-up made by first time financial backers is to find the property first, then, at that point, get supporting. Before you go out to track down that unlikely treasure, get pre-supported for funding. Settle on a moneylender by picking a bank, contract organization or online credit organization. While chatting with your bank, let them know the amount you are hoping to contribute. They'll accumulate loads of monetary data about you - pay, record of loan repayment, liabilities - and provide you with a thought of the amount they'll back. With the a wide range of funding decisions accessible today, you'll have to conclude which choice turns out best for you. Funding plans have various factors including various rates, beginning money venture, and expense suggestions.

3. Search for your property:-

Finding land that you can create a gain with can be interesting. Utilize the web and neighborhood paper's "Land" segment. Search for deserted and "For Lease" homes. Cruise all over the area you're keen on and attempt to find "Available to be purchased by Proprietor" properties.

4. Arrange a fair arrangement:-

Whenever you've found the ideal house, you'll have to haggle at the best cost. Try not to expect that you'll get a take. Venders are attempting to the most cash for their property, and purchasers are attempting to pay the least sum. Haggling great includes cooperating with the vender to find a mutually beneficial arrangement. Be decisive, yet plan to make concessions. Resoluteness frequently creates costly setbacks and added pressure.

Benefitting in Land

One report demonstrates that more than 23% of all out home deals in 2004 were purchased as speculation properties. This isn't a shock, since home costs have had a high rate expansion lately and the market has been encountering exceptional yields.

There are numerous ways of bringing in cash putting resources into land. "Flipping" a property implies that you get it, fix it up rapidly, and exchange it for a benefit.

Dispossessions are one more method for getting speculation property, which is the point at which a property holder defaults on a credit and the home loan holder then, at that point, puts it available to be purchased.

With leave property, it's not unexpected indistinct who holds the title to the property, so there's broad title research and legitimate work that happens with these properties. Paper ventures, or non-property land speculations, are the point at which you put resources into a common assets or security that is straightforwardly connected with the housing market, yet not genuine property. These speculations ought to be made with exhortation of an expert merchant.

Deal with Your Openness

Dealing with the gamble related with putting resources into land is critical to shielding yourself from misfortune. The main part of chance administration in land is to know the law. It's fundamental that you have a functioning information on the land lawful construction and prerequisites.

After you've investigated property accessibility, cost, and purchaser premium, you'll have to conjecture about what's on the horizon for your market. Will costs go up or down?

While thinking about your gamble, remember the accompanying focuses:

- **Contemplate the neighborhood economy:-**

Are there occupations accessible or are most organizations in the space losing positions? Are new homes being fabricated pretty much than throughout the course of recent years?

- **Settle on savvy funding decisions:-**

While picking your source of financial support, contemplate how long you intend to keep the property. Movable Rate Home loans (ARMs) are alluring a direct result of their lower initial installments and lower rates. You can pick the term of the credit - commonly either 1,5, or long term ARMs - and your rate will be acclimated to the overarching rates after this timeframe. On the off chance that you intend to clutch a property longer than the ARM, ARMs can set you back more in view of the greater loan fees. It could be more reasonable to decide on a decent rate contract with the most brief length you can deal with monetarily.

- **Pay an enormous up front installment to decrease your gamble:-**

On the off chance that you can put down 10%, you'll have moment value in the property, and in all likelihood get a superior loan fee.

- **Be inventive with your home loan installments:-**

Make bigger regularly scheduled installments then require, or make an additional one installment a year you'll diminish your rule.

Getting the Best yield

To get the most potential cash-flow in land, the standard way of thinking is to "purchase low, sell high". The vast majority attempt to do this, and many don't succeed on the grounds that it's difficult to do. While attempting to get the best yield conceivable, minimize your expenses and do all that could be within reach to attract the most noteworthy bidders.

When you own the property, do as a large part of the maintenance work yourself, for however long it is of an expert level. Poor work and second rate materials will cost more to address later. With troublesome undertakings, recruit a prepared proficient from a limited scale activity. Huge workers for hire with a few representatives need to figure their enormous above their costs.

While hoping to amplify your benefits, attempt to set aside cash with your bank. Search for less expensive advances with the less famous moneylenders. The huge banks and supporting organizations normally have high charges and rates. Try not to acknowledge overrated expenses. For instance, your moneylender is charging $75 to convey a couple of papers a brief distance, request it to be decreased.

By teaching yourself on the legitimate and bookkeeping parts of land exchanges, you can save yourself great many dollars. On the off chance that you become familiar with the fundamentals of these two regions you will know when to request an expert's assistance.

While arranging, be firm yet adaptable. Endeavor to find a mutually beneficial arrangement where both you and the other party leave the table cheerful. Be sure about what you need, and what you can be adaptable on. In the event that the other party leaves irate and feeling cheated, they could attempt to undermine your endeavor to create a gain.

Assuming you are selling your property, it's critical to likewise search around and haggle at the best costs on extravagant things, land commissions, and shutting costs.

"Organizing" is laying the right foundation by making your property put its best self forward. You will get the greatest cost for a property that has been appropriately arranged.

Effectively market your property and you'll get the biggest pool of potential purchasers conceivable. It is an advantage to the vender in the event that there are a few closely involved individuals in your property.

Trade with flawless timing

Timing is significant in all ventures, yet in contrast to different speculations - securities, stocks, and shared assets to give some examples - there are two qualities well defined for land effective financial planning.

- Land exchanges consume most of the day.

- Each piece of land is one of a kind.

To trade property it requires a long investment, and keeping in mind that the exchange is occurring, the market is continually evolving. This makes timing the buy or offer of land interesting. At the point when you are putting resources into land, you are attempting to sell high and afterward bounce once more into the market by purchasing low. Timing the market in such a manner is a test.

Search for property that is a "project" to get a reasonable setup. On the off chance that you have a fitness for home fix or you know an economical specialist, you can build the worth of a home by more than 10%. Look for dispossession sell-offs and Notice of Default cautions in the space papers and on the web. Track down a fair plan on property by expecting positive change in discouraged regions. Anticipated areas, in regions where individuals have been leaving will generally have lower costs. Find regions where the public authority is associated with advancement endeavors.

The way to utilizing any of these techniques is the admittance to capital. This doesn't mean having a record with an enormous amount of cash in it. All things considered, you want to approach cash. By keeping a high FICO rating, supporting a productive relationship with your loan specialist for speedy endorsement for funding, and approaching fluid resources, you'll be ready to bounce when the right arrangement goes along.

Indeed, even in a sluggish market, the opportunity to create a gain putting resources into land is still probable. To do this, in any case, you'll have to get your work done, have a drawn out viewpoint, and have the option to leave any arrangement.

Setting aside Money on Seemingly insignificant details Adds Up

Purchasing property is perhaps of the biggest buy you'll at any point make. Regardless of whether you're not setting up an enormous up front installment, by having a home loan you are making yourself liable for a sizable measure of cash. There's additionally the chance of assessment outcomes.

By setting aside as much money as possible, you'll have cash for the things that definitely spring up. For what it's worth, you realize you'll have to pay for the shutting costs and the underlying up front installment. Shutting costs incorporate the home loan, fire and risk protection, title expenses, and numerous other exorbitant things.

Follow these tips to set aside cash:

Get the best funding bargain you can find

Above all else, make certain to have your funding set up before you make a proposition. To get the best arrangement, research the rates that anyone could hope to find for your FICO assessment and attempt to get funding organizations to seek your business. Ask what choices are accessible given your FICO score. Haggle with your bank to lower or wipe out exorbitant expenses and charges. Try not to pay an application charge if possible.

Track down your own suppliers

You don't need to utilize the organizations that your representative or loan specialist suggest. This is significant while choosing your title and insurance agency. Your representative and bank have arrangements of suggested organizations since they have pre-laid out connections. Remember that you are the one paying them. Cautiously survey their charges and rates prior to pursuing a choice. You can utilize any organization you wish.

Arrange

Indeed, even a vender in a seasonally tight market should be adaptable. Individuals sell for some reasons - passing in the family, separate, work moves, and so on. Dealers in these circumstances are exceptionally energetic to finish the land exchange rapidly at practically any expense. On the off chance that you're willing to work with them and be adaptable, you might get a reasonable setup.

Chapter 2

The Land Deals Cycle

About Flipping

Purchasing land and selling it again quick, and in a perfect world for a benefit, is classified "flipping". This sort of land effective financial planning is totally legitimate and moral. Pessimistic press over flipping land most likely comes from media inclusion of land misrepresentation circumstances, where individuals have deliberately overrated the market worth of a home, deceitfully finished reports, or worked with others to exploit a purchaser. No part of this occurs in a legit flip.

Finding a property that is a decent flip requires a couple of aggressive strides on your part. You'll be looking, in all likelihood, for an under valued home needing fix. Or on the other hand you will be searching for a merchant that needs to sell quick, subsequently getting you a lower cost.

One method for finding property drives is to converse with companions, family, business partners, realtors, or brokers. Go out to the local you're thinking about and search for "Available to be purchased by Proprietor" signs, or ring doorbells to check whether anybody in the space is thinking about selling.

Check the public land records and search for "fire deals". This typically implies that the proprietor of the property is experiencing issues making contract installments. On the off chance that you reach them and they consent to sell, you're helping them out of their troublesome monetary circumstance. Furthermore, you're getting a property that might create a gain. Whenever done consciously, there's nothing deceptive about this exchange.

To be a fruitful land flipper, you should level up or foster numerous abilities. You should have an eye for the gem waiting to be discovered. You ought to have the option to evaluate purchasers precisely. It is ideal in the event that you are convenient and can bring care of fundamental back home fixes. It is vital that you are meticulous and a multi-

entrusting project supervisor. Flipping includes many subtleties, and it means a lot to be on time with the task to stay away from exorbitant deferrals. Ultimately, you should have predominant relational abilities.

Plan to hold the administrations of an expert bookkeeper, except if you are adequate at these abilities. Likewise find a decent legal counselor who can furnish you with legitimate guidance.

Tracking down Funding - Innovative Thoughts

For a long time, the method for supporting land was to make a 20% initial investment, and get a credit for the excess 80%. Obviously you could make a higher up front installment, yet 20% was ordinarily the base. Fortunately, this standard has changed.

There are currently a few money choices accessible to the land financial backer. One well known method for funding your buy is to have a subsequent home loan. The purchaser makes a 5% initial investment, and gets the excess 15%, generally at a higher financing cost, on an alternate credit.

Despite the fact that it's good to contribute less on a property, the higher loan cost isn't the main disadvantage. For the most part, in the event that the purchaser doesn't meet the 20% least, they are expected to get exorbitant confidential home loan protection (PMI).

You can eliminate PMI when the advance to-esteem (LTV) proportion comes to 80%. This is accomplished by settling the subsequent home loan and enthusiasm for the property estimation. This doesn't occur frequently on the grounds that the property is generally sold or the purchaser renegotiates before PMI can be eliminated.

For innovative financial backers, other funding sources exist. Makers of homes in arranged advancements are much of the time ready to give funding to early purchasers.

One more unsafe and rather confounded approach to supporting a property is called 'sub2' which means 'subject-to'. This sort of arrangement is the point at which the vender gives you the deed to the property, the credit stays set up, yet the purchaser never lawfully assumes control over the advance, simply the installments. There are a wide range of forms of this sort of exchange. Due to the intricacy and chance, this strategy for financing a venture isn't suggested for novices.

You can likewise consider shaping a restricted organization to fund your land venture. There are a wide range of plans on this strategy. A few kinds affect every individual in the organization contributing in a piece of the expense, generally half each. Be that as it may, once in a while the benefit is conveyed comparative with the first sum contributed. Another game plan is that one portion of the organization contributes the capital, and the other half offers the required types of assistance, for example, fixes on a home that should be fixed. There are a wide range of varieties of this strategy.

Government advances are accessible to low pay financial backers, or purchasers who have served in the military. These projects are typically just accessible for main living places.

Did you at any point ponder purchasing a home on a Mastercard? This is one more strategy for supporting your land buy, despite the fact that it's normally not suggested. Clearly, the financing costs on most Visas are significantly higher than credit rates. Another disadvantage is that banks decide your financial soundness in light of your remarkable obligation, and assuming you use Visa loans to cover the 5-20% up front installment that you want, you'll likely get turned down for a credit. This is likewise valid for cash acquired from companions or family, except you can show that the cash is really a gift.

The Bank's Point of view on Advancing Cash

Loan specialists are occupied with loaning individuals cash since they settle on painstakingly determined choices in view of your gamble. They have two assumptions;

that you will reimburse them and that they will create a gain. To pass judgment assuming that you are equipped for meeting those two models, banks check out intently at your ongoing monetary position and your verifiable monetary circumstance.

While passing judgment on your monetary past, banks will check out:

Record of loan repayment

They'll survey the size and number of past credits and the reimbursement history on those advances. They'll likewise take a gander at your credit ratings and different other crude information.

Pay history

What is your benefit history on your different speculations?

Over what time allotment? They'll take a gander at the most recent three years of pay explanations and expense forms, your obligation, and any lawful decisions that might influence your monetary standing.

Your involvement in advances

Essentially, the bank needs to realize that you are reliable and will hold up your finish of the credit understanding. This implies you should be dependable and settle on great business choices.

Current property and monetary circumstance

Loan specialists are most keen on liquidity - your income and pay.

At the point when moneylenders are taking a gander at your capacity to create a gain, they'll need to realize about your complete costs connected with the property. What amount will it cost you to deal with the property?

What will your protection rates, assessments, and cost of fixes be? The loan specialist needs to see that you can take care of your expenses related with house purchasing, as well as their advantage charges.

Loan specialists frequently need short reimbursement periods, while it normally more valuable for the purchaser to have longer periods. Longer reimbursement periods imply that you can keep away from beginning expenses, extra examination charges, and different expenses. With regards to credits for speculation property, a long term fixed rate advance is viewed as a long advance. Regularly this incorporates an inflatable installment five to a decade into the credit.

Assuming your loan specialist attempts to drive you into a more limited reimbursement period, you can set up a game plan that you re-cost following five years, rather than paying a lot of money in one singular amount. A typical option is the overall prime loan fee in addition to 1%.

Remember that most things in land financial planning are debatable, and that your loan specialist can be your accomplice in land money management. Fostering a positive long haul working relationship with your lender can help you.

Chasing after Your Unlikely treasure

Indeed, even in major areas of strength for a with the new innovation accessible to surrender to-the-minute evaluations of properties, a financial backer can lose a lot of cash in a brief timeframe. For the most obvious opportunity to fruitful get your ideal speculation property, think about these ideas:

Exploit the web

You can see as a "unlikely treasure" via looking through the large numbers of properties recorded on the web, and survey the property's portrayal, pictures, asking cost, and lawful data. Typically, the best way to stay away from a realtor expense is to search for property recorded Available to be purchased by Proprietor, or posted on other free locales.

Investigate getting your own admittance to the Numerous Posting Administration (MLS)

A permit is expected in certain region, however a few spots you can get involved with the help for a charge.

Get out and research the region that you're thinking about purchasing face to face

Will the cost be held down in view of the state of the area?

If conceivable, converse with the neighbors. They could surrender data about the property that the dealer hasn't notice, similar to the front yard that floods following two days of downpour.

Get an expert review

At the point when you make your proposition, add a good home review possibility. Utilize a confided in proficient overseer and cautiously survey the definite examination report. Not many properties, even new development, are awesome. Utilize the report to arrange the maintenance of issues or a change in accordance with the selling cost.

The Significance of the Home Assessment

The state of land is different in each circumstance. To safeguard yourself while making such a significant speculation, having an exhaustive review by a prepared professional is significant. Make your proposal to buy property dependent upon a good home review, and you will try not to put resources into a cash pit.

What precisely is thought of "palatable"? Any home containing wood ought to have a bug review, where the monitor searches for proof of harm brought about by termites, mice, craftsman subterranean insects or different irritations. This review is discrete from that done by the home assessor.

Your home overseer ought to zero in on each mechanical and primary part of the property. They will search for significant breaks in the establishment, levelness of the construction, and dampness in the storm cellar. Water infiltration is obvious when there is form, mold or blooming - a white powder that shows where water has entered. Innovative overseers use lasers to check whether the things are level and concentrated radon gas meters to decide whether there is a radon gas issue.

The design of the house is firmly assessed. Homes lay on top of an establishment. Floors have been introduced on top of this establishment, and it should be assessed to guarantee that appropriate materials have been utilized. Then, the walls could have ill-advised outlining or conceivable harm from water. Electrical and plumbing frameworks exist in the walls, and where conceivable, these inside frameworks are assessed for wear, out-of-code development, and harm. Pipes are investigated for holes or synthetic worries like lead or rust. A few home reviewers test the water tension and stream pace of the house.

The home's electrical framework is totally examined. The controller searches for revealed switches or outlets, mistaken wiring, inadequate establishing, defective circuit breakers, or unsuitable GFCI trips.

Once in the loft, the examiner ought to check for water harm and air spills. The outlining is taken a gander at to guarantee that it is solid. The underside of the rooftop is investigated for a decent seal where vent pipes go through the rooftop.

On the rooftop, the monitor looks at it for openings, free shingles or tile, unfortunate blazing, or whatever other worry that could make the rooftop not hold facing the components.

Warming and cooling frameworks are assessed for satisfactory stream, pipe holes, and channel condition. Outside fixtures are tried to be certain they work and don't release or have insufficient water stream.

All apparatuses included with the offer of the house are analyzed. The heated water tank, oven, wood ovens and some other underlying units are check for appropriate capability and norms consistence.

This data is all accumulated in the exhaustive assessment report that is accessible to the individual or organization that paid for the review. Reviews benefit the purchaser since they can involve issues with the property as negotiating tools during talks. The home review is additionally advantageous to the dealer since they then get a legitimate evaluation of the state of their property and can make enhancements to certain things prior to putting their home available to be purchased.

The home examination is one region where two or three hundred bucks burned through frequently saves large number of dollars during the buy interaction.

Limit your Gamble with Protection

In 2005, the middle home cost rose practically 15% over the earlier year, and, surprisingly, more in some housing markets. The base required FICO (financial assessment) was brought down, a portion of the documentation prerequisites were diminished, and the remittance for obligation was expanded to 45% of pay. It is assessed that 30% of all new home loans are interest-just home loans. Practically 35% of home advances are Movable Rate Home loans (ARMs). Beginning in June 2004, the Central bank has raised financing costs multiple times.

These details demonstrate that there has been amazing development in the housing market over late years. As the home costs have risen, so has the partner risk implied with trading property. Fortunately, every kind of chance currently has a fitting protection. Of all, the two most famous are title and risk protection.

Title protection guarantees the inclusion of any potential monetary misfortune that is a consequence of a mistake in the handling and exploring of a property title. Any failures that could occur during the title search process, preceding shutting, are covered. The title organization will look through an openly available report information base to ensure that the property can be sold, meaning it's liberated from encumbrances. Freely available reports are not generally totally precise, and blunders can happen.

Risk protection covers wounds that occur on, or in light of, the property. Assuming somebody slips and falls on your property, your risk protection would give inclusion. The more inclusion you have, the more costly it becomes.

Danger protection is accessible for more uncertain dangers like storms, flooding, or tremors.

You can likewise get inclusion for mishaps made by people. This incorporates synthetic spills, electrical glitches, defacement, robbery, and so forth.

It's ideal to look for good rates, and give close consideration to your deductible sum, and any limits on the strategy.

Fixing the Property Receives Monetary Benefits

The most ideal way to improve the probability that you'd get as much as possible for your property is to set it up. You don't need to be a coach handyman or craftsman to make your home more appealing to purchasers. With only a couple of devices and some difficult work you can give your property a very much kept up with appearance.

It's really smart to go through the house and make minor fixes prior to showing it, or putting it available. A home review will probably be finished before the last arrangement, so in the event that you require some investment front and center to make the minor fixes, you'll have the option to stay away from a portion of the potential purchaser's negotiating concessions in arranging an arrangement. Fix the cracked washroom spigot and fix broken windows.

Deal with your property's control advance. Keep up with the arranging by managing the yard and bushes, and establishing a few blossoms. The beyond the house will attract forthcoming purchasers, or keep them driving.

Request that your neighbors tidy up their yard; propose to remove their garbage and garbage for them, request that they move youngster's toys, or propose to cut the yards close to your property. You might really think about giving a little money motivation after the effective offer of the home.

Your home ought to be really perfect before you show it. It's generally excessively costly to supplant all the covering in a home, yet getting it cleaned is reasonable. Place your furniture in manners that cover worn spots. Put down new doormats and supplant worn region carpets. Wash every one of the windows until they shimmer. Fix worn conductor, and supplant air channels on cooling and warming for a new look. Provide the walls with a new layer of paint.

Be certain the work looks expertly finished, so that individuals can see the nature of your property. A very much kept up with home generally collects a higher deals cost than a home that has been disregarded.

Selling it Yourself, or Utilize a Specialist?

Selling your home yourself, likewise called FSBO or Available to be purchased by Proprietor, is a sensible choice on account of the web. Individuals sell their own property without a specialist since they keep away from exorbitant realtor commissions. This commission is commonly around 6% of the property deal cost. Specialists really buckle down for their payments, and give significant knowledge into the market and deals process.

They ordinarily have important experience selling different properties nearby. Assuming you sell it yourself, you stand to save large number of dollars, however you are taking on everything that the realtor does. Is selling your property FSBO appropriate for you? Contemplate these focuses while settling on this choice:

Evaluating it right the initial time

To value your property accurately, you want to know the market. An unfortunate estimating choice can cost you - under valuing will bring about lost possible profit, and over evaluating will make the home sit available while you are paying costly conveying costs. Home costs change contingent upon the area, parcel size, age, and different elements. Use neighborhood comparables to pass judgment on the most fitting rundown cost.

Spread the news

Assuming that you sell FSBO, you will not approach the biggest, most important showcasing instrument, the MLS. Yet, because of the web, the MLS isn't the best way to showcase your home. Put out signs, show it on sites, and spot advertisements in the paper to tell purchasers about your home.

Could you at any point haggle effectively?

Certain individuals are brought into the world with this ability, and other need to work at it. On the off chance that you are not a carefully prepared land mediator, research the subject and learn sufficient about it to try not to lose cash.

Be a quick learner

You'll have to do what a specialist does. Find out about the deals cycle, lawful issues, contracts, shutting interaction, protection, and numerous different parts of the selling land.

Tolerance is significant

Selling FSBO is a ton of work and little subtleties, and you are responsible for overseeing them to take care of business.

Going with the choice to do it without anyone else's help can be fulfilling and set aside a ton of cash, yet an indifferent endeavored will probably be fruitless.

Promoting Plan Advancement and Execution

Like it or not, you normally need to invest energy advertising your property for it to sell. What is promoting? Promoting is the production of a procedure used to sell a thing. Research, advancement, promoting and deals are all important for advertising.

Research your neighborhood market, and the costs at which comparables sell. You'll have to have your finger on the beat of the market during the whole deals process, which can require months. This is significant in light of the fact that you might be in talks over an extensive stretch of time, and knowing the expert remaining of your property will assist you with pursuing taught exchange choices.

Promoting is expected to arrange a huge gathering of intrigued purchasers. By hosting numerous gatherings that need to buy your property you might have the option to make an offering war which will drive up the deal cost. How could you publicize? Utilize all of your publicizing assets, similar to the paper, verbal, flyers, designated mailings, exceptional exchange booklets, and the web.

The web is one of the best ways of showcasing. There are numerous land speculation sites that permit you to post your property with pictures. A thorough promoting effort incorporates these web based showcasing instruments. Track down a site with great traffic and incorporate complimenting photographs of the inside and outside of your property. You can consider adding a virtual visit.

On the off chance that It's Not Selling Rapidly Enough

Housing markets go through cycles. Depending where in the cycle you will be, you might think that it is simple, or troublesome, to sell your speculation property. On the off chance that the market has hit a level or gone down, you could need to hang tight for purchasers. This will tie up cash and cause you to need to stand by to create a gain, which can baffle.

There are a couple of procedures you can use to get yourself out of this sort of circumstance.

- On the off chance that it's your main living place and you can stand to do as such, endure it. The market normally changes each 1 to 5 years, and you can sell on the following rise.

- Check out at your property according to the perspective of the purchaser and make every single essential improvement. This will make your property more alluring to purchasers. Consider what may be an obstruction and record for it. For instance, on the off chance that you live close to a noisy thruway, close the windows and play delicate music to detract from this disadvantage.

- Stage the house. Set out a couple of bunches of roses, turn the lights on, put on some light ambient sound, prepare a few new treats for a warm smell and invited snacks for guests. Put out a flyer on the property with a lot of appealing pictures, an indication of the property features and your contact data. Work everything out such that the purchaser can see themselves living there. Purchasers need a home they that does right by them.

- Urge your neighbors to assist you with working on the presence of the area.

- Ensure you've evaluated the home accurately. Markets shift every now and again, so you probably won't be valued seriously evaluated for the ongoing business sector.

Assuming you've attempted these tips and the property has still not sold, have a go at taking it off the market for a little while, and afterward show it again after re-really looking at your valuing. At the point when houses sit available too lengthy, potential purchasers expect there should be an off-base thing. Broadly promote your property. Putting forth the additional attempt to get your home sold will just assist you with creating a gain.

Arranging a Mutually beneficial Arrangement

While arranging, arm yourself with data and information and you will be exceptional to handle a fair arrangement. Find out however much you can about genuine bequest regulation, the ongoing business sector, and the other individual's circumstance. Assuming you are purchasing the house figure out why they are selling. Is it true or not that they are in abandonment? Has something happened actually that makes them anxious to dispose of the property at any sensible cost? Figure out how long the put has been available, the quantity of different offers, if any, and at what sum. Is there exceptional obligation on the home, and assuming this is the case how much? Might it be said that they are fully informed regarding their installments?

Most venders won't simply give out this data. Attempt to decide their status by surrendering your very own piece data first. Be cautious about what you say in light of the fact that the dealer could possibly utilize it while haggling with you later.

At the point when you are locked in with the other party in arranging an agreement, you're attempting to come to a common settlement on the cost of the property and terms. Consider the region comps, genuine state of the property from the assessment report, and dealer's circumstance. Prior to engaging in any discussion have your supporting set up by being pre-endorsed. Prior to marking any composed offers or agreements, look for lawful insight.

Chapter 3

Different Contemplations in Effective money management

Know the Land Regulation

All aspects of land includes the law. There are many confounded legitimate pieces and a wide range of individuals are engaged with any land exchange.

The agreement, first and foremost, is most significant piece of trading property. The main role of an agreement is to show common consent - the understanding by the two players to the trade recorded as a hard copy. Verbal arrangements are not restricting. To be legitimate an agreement, it should incorporate the accompanying:

- Recognizable proof of the gatherings in question and the settled upon cost

- Explicit "thought" should be expressed - something of significant worth that is being traded, typically cash

- Marks of each party included

There are governing rules to safeguard individuals in each circumstance and to safeguard the general framework. Examinations are utilized to guarantee that the property is worth what the bank and dealer have implied. The examination forestalls obscure arrangements being stuck among financial backers and home loan merchants. Business property has its own regulations in regards to utilize and deal. On the off chance that there are occupants living in the property, there are explicit regulations to safeguard the landowner and occupants. Banks are held to the law by the amount they can credit, what records and protection are required, and even the way that they market their funding programs.

It's vital to be familiar with charge regulation, or get guidance from an expert, since it extraordinarily influences your progress in land effective money management.

Botches are exorbitant, and by safeguarding yourself you can pursue choices that will help your main concern as opposed to remove your benefits.

Contributing Expense Suggestions

Prior to covering the subject of land charge regulation, comprehend that the accompanying ought not be considered legitimate guidance. Look for lawful guidance from your lawyer or bookkeeper while going with any legitimate or burden choices.

Every region has its own duty codes, yet the following are a couple of general tips to consider that apply in many areas:

- You can sell your main living place tax-exempt on the off chance that you've resided there for at least two years. Speculation property that has been sold is dependent upon capital increases charge, and whenever held for short of what one year, it's at the normal personal expense rates which can be all around as high as 35%. In the event that the property is held one year or more prior to selling, it's viewed as a drawn out capital increase and is normally charged at 15%.

- You can likewise sell tax-exempt in the event that you save the property as a home for 730 days, not really in succession. On the off chance that you sell and reinvest the money into a home of equivalent or more prominent worth, you won't have to cover charge.

- "Like kind" speculation exchanges, otherwise called the 1031 trade, can be utilized to concede charges. You can utilize this to exchange lacking area for property with a house, a rental home for a business building, and so on. You can require 45 days to situate up to 3 substitute properties, and you should have the end in 180 days or less. You likewise need to hold a facilitator, or nonpartisan party, to keep exact records and hold the cash.

You can't do a 1031 trade with your main living place.

- Contract interest can be deducted from your charges. Advances esteemed at up to $1 million are qualified, and start expenses and focuses can be incorporated.

Since the expense regulation is so confounded, it's ideal to look for proficient help whenever you are in a circumstance that is strange. The sum you pay for their administrations will be saved ten times by their mastery in the field.

The Advantages and disadvantages of Provincial versus Metropolitan Speculations

One land pattern is the shift of purchasers from populated metropolitan areas to less populated provincial spots. Novel properties like grape plantations, Bed and Morning meals, horse ranches, and agrarian homesteads, have acknowledged expanded property estimations thanks to some extent to maturing, monetarily secure, children of post war America. Albeit these areas are attractive while putting resources into land, there are a few difficulties related with country properties.

Finding a property can be a test. With the expanded ubiquity of individuals telecommuting, and more retired folks searching for provincial retreats, it very well may be challenging to track down a venture property at a deal cost.

Finding solid and qualified workers for hire that are reasonable frequently presents a test in country areas. You might have to pay a premium for gifted work, regardless of whether the typical pay in the space is lower than in the city.

At the point when property is remarkable, it's hard to evaluate. Numerous provincial properties don't have sensible comps, so the worth is basically speculated. Banks know about this sort of circumstance, so they could to be less able to back a credit for a stand-out property. This typically isn't an issue on the off chance that the purchaser has strong credit and can give a more significant up front installment.

At the point when it comes time to sell a provincial venture property, you should showcase your property over a bigger region to arrange a gathering of intrigued, and qualified, possible purchasers.

Putting resources into Land Abandonments

While certain dispossessions might look interesting to the land financial backer, it's fundamental to consider many elements before you go into an arrangement including an abandoned property.

What is abandonment? A lawful interaction happens when a home loan holder reclaims a property when installments are not current.

By purchasing a dispossessed property, you are going into a legitimate wreck. Some abandonment circumstances take into account the 'right of recovery'. This implies that the land owner can make back installments and reclaim the title. Clearly, you need to avoid this. While considering a dispossession, search for circumstances where, at least, a Notification of Default has been given.

A special point about dispossessions is that the property is sold "with no guarantees". There are no guarantees and no title protection. Have an expert investigation ahead of time, and never make a proposal without taking a gander at the property by and by. In the event that there are issues with the property however you are searching for a house to fix, decrease your proposition fittingly. Prior to purchasing, lead a careful title search.

Two different kinds of dispossession are REO and 'short deal' bargains. REO means "land claimed". This is the point at which the moneylender possesses the property since it was unloaded, yet nobody got it. You can find a REO deal, yet be extremely cautious. The property as a rule wasn't accepted which is as it should be. Short deal bargains happen when a bank will take less cash than stays on the current credit.

Putting resources into Business Property

Business land speculation (CREI) represents a negligible part of all land ventures, with private property being the biggest section. Since it is a little slice of the pie doesn't mean it's less confounded.

Business property is most frequently purchased for business purposes as a venture. Regardless of whether it's an apartment complex with a few lofts, it's viewed as business.

While putting resources into business property, you need to put away more cash, which requires incredible credit. By putting more cash down, you have presented yourself to more serious gamble. Business financial backers additionally need to decide their

rate of return (rate of return) and Gross Lease Multiplier (GRM) to choose if a venture is a decent choice.

The rate of return and GRM are valuable computations while effective financial planning. The rate of return equation is: Yearly Net Working Pay/Price tag. Generally, a sound venture has a 8-10% rate of return. The lower the rate, the higher the gamble and the lower the expected benefit. The equation used to compute the GRM is: Price tag/Month to month Gross Working Pay.

You ought to likewise think about the property comps, examination versus evaluation, pay and substitution costs while considering on the off chance that an arrangement is worth the effort.

Business properties are additionally interesting in light of the fact that the financial states of an area frequently direct the inhabitance of business property.

While purchasing business property, you'll have to initially teach yourself on region drafting, renting rules, business regulation, building support, and other legitimate issues. Since the property will no doubt be leased, you'll have to think about fire wellbeing, web and phone capacities, more mind boggling plumbing and electrical necessities, security frameworks, and that's only the tip of the iceberg. Just when a property manager has a triple-net rent - where the inhabitant pays for and organizes all upkeep, fixes, and protection will the inclusion be less.

Obviously a benefit can be produced using CREI. In spite of the fact that there are more dangers, the potential benefit is frequently higher.

The Upsides and downsides of Leasing Property

Some of the time financial backers clutch property with the expectations of creating a gain through rental, while profiting from the capital appreciation and helpful duty code.

While choosing whether to hold or sell a property, compute out your assessed charges in the event that you keep the property, as opposed to selling it. Speculate about future deals costs are going in light of loan fees, patterns, and the ongoing business sector.

On the off chance that you've chosen to turn into a landowner, remember the accompanying:

- Have all candidates total an application. Utilize this data to direct a total historical verification; survey rental and record, and converse with their references, past property managers and bosses.

- Utilize an agreement that is straightforward and is fair. It ought to incorporate data about the sum and limitations of the store, under what conditions and how much notification is required for the landowner to enter the rental, who is answerable for what, and so on.

- Do what you say, and then some. Keep your occupants cheerful and odds are good that they'll pay the lease. Assuming you're delayed to answer support demands or don't keep up the property, they could quit paying rent.

- In the event that an occupant is late with the lease, figure out why immediately. Urge them to have the lease paid by the due date by helping them to remember the late charge condition in the rent. Keep clear records of installments since you might require this data on the off chance that lawful activity were at any point required.

- Assuming you really do have to make a lawful move, attempt to initially go through mediation. Cases are commonly dealt with quicker and all the more proficiently.

Elective Land Speculation Instruments

There are ways of putting resources into land while never managing the bare essential pieces of the business - no review, examination, or promoting. Land Monetary Trusts (REITs), Home loan Supported Protections (MBS), and Independent IRAs are approaches to putting resources into land on paper alone.

Land Monetary Trusts (REITs) are shared assets that attention on land; speculations are made in both actual property and home loan portfolios. It's taken care of like different protections and has extraordinary expense circumstances. REITs frequently have

improved yields and give more straightforward admittance to cash than conventional property speculation.

There are Home loan, Value, and Mixture REITs. Contract REITs put resources into contracts, with income coming from the home loan interest. Value REITs own and put resources into genuine land, with the greater part of the income coming from rental pay. Crossover REITs are a blend of both.

Very much like other common assets, when bought they can't be traded out through the asset, however must be offered to one more financial backer through a specialist.

REITs can be viewed as high return, since profits are paid out to investors at 90% or a greater amount of available income. Profits in addition to appreciation approaches the all out return, and REITs are similar to little cover stock in that around 66% of the return comes from the profits. Accordingly, REITs are affected by changes in loan costs. At the point when loan costs increment, the cost of REITs typically decline.

Contract Back Protections are bonds upheld by a gathering of home loan credits. Very much like other sort of securities, you procure a coupon pace of interest. In contrast to different bonds, notwithstanding, financial backers get reimbursements of the guideline in little parts, over the span of the MBS, as the home loan advances that back the MBS are paid off, rather than in one single amount when the security develops.

One reason that the MBS is a steady venture is on the grounds that there are such countless credits in the pool; the couple of credits that default or pay off early don't dispense with the financial backer's benefit.

While picking either short MBS and pre-payable MBS, decide whether loan costs are probably going to rise or fall. Contract holders can pre-pay their home loans, and assuming that financing costs drop individuals will renegotiate to exploit better rates, the two situations will adversely affect the MBS financial backer. On the off chance that financing costs are supposed to drop, a short MBS is the better choice.

A Personally managed Individual Retirement Record (IRA) can hold resources like land, single family homes, and business property rather than simply cash.

Before you put resources into any land venture, contact a monetary expert and do your own exploration to pursue the most ideal choice for you.

Conclusion

Land is a diverse, extravagant industry. As a financial backer, it's vital to know the business and proceed with a reasonable plans of action to make money. From every venture experience you will acquire significant abilities that you can apply to future financial planning attempts.

www.ingramcontent.com/pod-product-compliance
Lightning Source LLC
Chambersburg PA
CBHW070245220526
45465CB00004B/1535